People of Destiny

A Humanities Series

There comes a time,
we know not when,
that marks
the destiny of men.

Joseph Addison Alexander

People of Destiny

CHARLES LINDBERGH

By Kenneth G. Richards

CHILDRENS PRESS, CHICAGO

*The editors wish to express
their appreciation to Mr. Meyer Goldberg,
who created the series and inspired
the publication of* People of Destiny

Cover and body design: John Hollis

Project editor: Joan Downing

*Illustrations: Harley Shelton—Hollis
Associates*

Research editor: Robert Hendrickson

*Photographs: From the files of Wide World
Photos, Inc. and Brown Brothers.*

Typesetting: American Typesetting Co.

Printing: Regensteiner Press

Quotations from The Spirit of St. Louis *by Charles Lindbergh on
pages 11, 12, 17, 18, 22, 30, 32, 33, 35, 37, 44, 55, 61, 62, are used
by permission of Charles Scribner's Sons, New York, and John
Murray, Ltd., London. Copyright 1953 Charles Scribner's Sons.
Quotations on pages 16, 25, 26, 41, 43, and 46 from* We *by Charles
Lindbergh, published by G. P. Putnam's Sons, New York, 1927.*

2 3 4 5 6 7 8 9 10 11 12 13 14 15 16 17 18 19 20 21 22 23 24 25   R   75 74 73 72 71 70 69

Contents

Wings of Destiny

The first streaks of dawn filtered through a scudding overcast at Roosevelt Field on Long Island. On this damp morning of May 20, 1927, a small crowd of people had gathered to watch an airplane takeoff. They also were here to bid *bon voyage* to the young pilot—whom many felt they would never see again.

It was not the airplane which had attracted the crowd—nor even the pilot, really. There was nothing outwardly unusual about either of them. The airplane, although it was the only one of its kind in the world, did not look very different from many other planes of its day. Painted on its nose was the name *Spirit of St. Louis*.

Many people said the pilot looked like the "typical American boy." He was over six feet tall, with broad shoulders and a frame so lean he was nicknamed "Slim." Only twenty-five years old, he was a handsome young man with light curly hair and a rare, but infectious, grin. Within two days the name of this "typical" young American would be on the lips of millions of people around the world. His name was Charles Augustus Lindbergh.

Lindbergh is shown here with protective helmet and goggles, ready for a flight.

On this Friday morning, relatively few people in the world had heard of Charles Lindbergh and his *Spirit of St. Louis*. Some people were aware that a "flying fool" was planning to try for the coveted Orteig prize of $25,000 for the first aviator to fly non-stop from New York to Paris. Others had already tried. Even now, ships were searching the vastness of the North Atlantic for two French pilots long overdue. And on this very field, a scorched circle of earth marked the spot where two men had burned to death when their overloaded plane had failed to become airborne in an ill-fated attempt at the elusive prize. People shook their heads in pity at the "crazy kid" who was now going to try it alone. They had little faith in his prospects for success.

But Charles Lindbergh had faith. He had watched this plane through every stage of its construction. He had worked alongside the builders at the Ryan factory in San Diego, suggesting modifications and poring endlessly over computations of weight, balance, gas load, tire stress, and a thousand other details. He had planned this journey with meticulous care. This "foolhardy" young man approached the crucial moment with the confidence that comes with sound and reasoned planning.

He was concerned, however, as he studied the runway conditions and wind direction. These were critical factors which could spell the difference between a successful takeoff and death. The unpaved runway was muddy. The muck and the standing pools of water might slow down the *Spirit of St. Louis* as it tried to gather enough speed to become airborne. At the other end of the field there were telephone wires to be cleared. There was no margin for error.

The airplane was also overweight. This was to be the first time that her gasoline tanks had been filled to capacity. The gross weight for this flight would exceed 5200 pounds—more than any engine of comparable size had ever lifted off the ground.

A good head wind, though, would help lift the plane off the runway. As mechanics started the engine for a check run, Lindbergh glanced at a wind sock on the roof of a nearby hangar. Instead of a helping head wind he had a tail wind. The scales of safety were tilted just a trifle more toward disaster.

For a brief moment Lindbergh paused as he weighed the odds. Should he postpone the flight and wait for better conditions? "This is the moment I've planned for, day and night, all these months past," he mused. "The decision is mine. No other man can take that responsibility. The mechanics, the engineers, the blue-uniformed police officers standing there behind the wing, everyone has done his part. Now, it's up to me."

He donned his flight suit over his army breeches and woolen sweater. With helmet and goggles on, he walked to the plane and climbed into the wicker seat in the cockpit. The mechanic who had been testing the engine yelled over the engine's noise, "She's thirty revolutions low. You have to expect that in this damp weather." The scales were tilted a fraction more.

Lindbergh ran the engine up to full throttle and the plane strained against the wheel chocks. After reading his instruments, he cut the throttle and leaned back in his wicker seat to make a last-minute evaluation of the situation.

For a moment, everything hinged on getting the *Spirit of St. Louis* safely airborne. The supreme test would come when the plane and its youthful pilot had safely cleared the telephone wires. Ahead lay a 3600-mile flight. Each mile would demand the greatest effort of man, plane, and engine. Each must operate at peak performance for a continuous day and a half. No sleep. No rest. Even the slightest malfunction of man or machine might bring disaster. But Charles Lindbergh was a meticulous planner. If he could get the *Spirit of St. Louis* safely off the ground he knew he would make it all the way.

Now, as he sat behind his idling engine he could . . ."turn to no formula, the limits of logic are now passed. Now, the intangible elements of flight—experience, instinct, intuition—must make the final judgment, place their weight upon the scales. In the last analysis, when the margin is close, when all the known factors have been considered,

after equations have produced their final lifeless numbers, one . . . checks the answer beyond the conscious mind."

For agonizingly long seconds, Lindbergh weighed all the factors. Then he buckled his safety belt, pulled down his goggles, and nodded his head to the men standing outside. The moment had come. The decision was made.

With a surge of power, the little plane began to creep forward. Men on either side began to push with all their might on the wing struts in an effort to speed the takeoff roll. The bulging tires mushed slowly through the mud as the plane sluggishly began to accelerate. Slowly but steadily the speed increased and one by one the men fell behind.

With his head peering out of the left side-window, Lindbergh concentrated on keeping the plane straight down the narrow runway. With the full tank of gas, the plane was slightly nose-heavy. Lindbergh struggled to keep the tail down. Puddles of water snatched at the speeding wheels and he kicked the rudder pedals to keep the *Spirit of St. Louis* pointed down the runway.

A stick with a white flag attached marked the point of no return. When he reached this marker he would have to make an instant decision as to whether to continue the takeoff. The white signal passed by in a blur of mist and the final, irrevocable decision was made.

Lindbergh allowed the tail to rise and the plane roared still faster down the muddy field. A rough spot bounced the plane into the air for an instant and Lindbergh eased forward on the control stick. The plane settled once again. There was a lightness now to the *Spirit of St. Louis* and it seemed ready to fly. The telephone lines were getting closer and closer as Lindbergh eased the stick back once more. Gradually the plane left the runway, poised precariously on the propeller's blast. The slightest twitch of the control stick or rudder pedals could upset the delicate balance and cause the plane to plunge to earth. Slim made a very gradual climb to build up speed. Then easily, gently, he steadied the wings and tugged the nose higher. The wires were coming faster now. They were past! By a bare twenty feet,

Lindbergh had skimmed the telephone lines. He was airborne at last.

The crowd at Roosevelt Field sent up a rousing cheer as the *Spirit of St. Louis* and its youthful pilot disappeared into the mists. The time was 7:52 A.M. Word was flashed to the world: "Lindbergh is on his way." With him went the prayers of an anxious nation. Many feared that the handsome young man would never be heard from again. Airplanes in 1927 were still regarded as unreliable machines strictly for the use of daredevils and military pilots. Commercial aviation was still in its infancy. The success of this flight would help prove the reliability of aircraft. If a lone man could fly all the way to Paris, perhaps the public attitude would change.

It was a mighty big "if." Ahead lay the perilous vastness of the Atlantic Ocean. Ahead, too, lay long hours of strain and fatigue that dulled the senses and numbed the mind. Charles Lindbergh would ride a path of danger where man had never been before. But he and his sturdy little airplane flew eastward to fame and honor on wings of destiny.

Ola Mansson, Charles Lindbergh's grandfather, was well known in his native Sweden. He had been born into hardship but had worked hard to advance from tenant farmer to landowner before becoming a member of the Riksdag (the Swedish parliament), a secretary to the king, and a close personal friend of the crown prince.

Ola however, was discontented with the social system in Sweden; he was angered by the lack of social reforms he felt were needed. Finally, he decided to bring his wife and newborn son to America. Just a year before the American Civil War began, the little family settled on the Minnesota frontier. The former parliamentarian became a hard-working pioneer. He built a log cabin, trapped and hunted in the forests, cleared and tilled the land, and fought the Indians.

After losing his arm in a sawmill accident, Ola designed scythes and tools which he fit into specially designed belts that enabled him to continue to work with only one arm. His courage and fortitude became legendary on the frontier.

When Ola Mansson decided to change his life and migrate to America, he also took a new name to make the change complete. The name he chose was August Lindbergh. His son, Charles, who grew up in the forests of Minnesota, named his boy Charles Augustus Lindbergh, Jr. Young Charles, the future "Lone Eagle," never knew his grandfather, who died ten years before Charles was born. But the tales of August Lindbergh's courage and resourcefulness thrilled and inspired the boy. Courage became a family tradition. Years later, these traits served Charles Lindbergh well on his flight with destiny.

Courage-A Family Trait

On February 4, 1902, an event occurred which would have little significance to the world for another quarter century. On that day, in Detroit, Michigan, C. A. and Evangeline Lindbergh became the parents of a healthy baby boy. The name they gave their son was destined to go down in history—Charles Augustus Lindbergh, Jr.

The future "Lone Eagle" was born into the Lindbergh tradition of courage, resourcefulness, and independence. Grandfather August Lindbergh had immigrated from Sweden half a century before. His courage had become legendary on the Minnesota frontier. Courage was, in fact, a Lindbergh family trait. From the Lands, his mother's family, the baby's heritage included a background of science and medicine. In future years, the boy would draw heavily upon these traditions and family traits.

When he was but a few weeks old, Charles was brought to the big house called "Lindholm" on the banks of the Mississippi River near Little Falls, Minnesota. Here, amid the quiet beauty of forests and meadows, he spent his first four and a half years. Then, one Sunday afternoon in August of 1906, tragedy struck the Lindbergh family. The beau-

tiful big house, and most of the furniture in it, burned to the ground. Fortunately, no one was injured. Young Charles was carried across the road to the barn and safety. A smaller house was soon built on the foundation of the old home.

Meanwhile, C. A. had run for election to Congress as a Republican representative from Minnesota's Sixth District. He was elected, and before the new house was completed, the Lindberghs were off to the nation's capital. As Charles himself would write later, "My father was elected to Congress and thereafter I seldom spent more than a few months in the same place." Throughout his youth, Charles did not attend any school for a full school year.

Being constantly on the move as he was, Charles never had a chance to develop close personal friends among his school chums. He did have two good friends in Little Falls, however, and when Congress was not in session, the family always returned to "Lindholm." With his friends Alex Johnson and Bill Thompson, Charles could spend the summer fishing and boating on the river.

At home in Minnesota, Charles loved to take long walks in the forests where not many years before the Chippewa

Charles, as a boy in Minnesota, built a raft on which he and his dog spent many hours exploring the Mississippi River.

and Sioux had made their trails. He enjoyed hunting with his father, who excited his imagination with tales of life on the old Minnesota frontier. Charles listened wide-eyed as his father recounted the legends of old August Lindbergh.

The boy also found pleasure in solitude. He built a raft and with only his spotted dog, Dingo, as a companion, he spent many quiet hours floating along the river and nearby streams. Sometimes he would land on a grassy bank and sprawl in the sun. The summers spent in Little Falls were among the happiest of his life. "I spent hours lying on my back in high timothy and redtop, hidden from passersby, watching white cumulus clouds drift overhead, staring into the sky. It was a different world up there. How wonderful it would be if I could fly up to the clouds and explore their caves and canyons . . . then I would ride on the wind and be part of the sky."

Life was completely different in Washington, D.C. There was a lot to do. Young Charles especially enjoyed the asphalt streets and sidewalks where he could zip around on roller skates. There was the Washington Monument to climb, government buildings to visit, and hiking and picnicking in Rock Creek

Park. Sometimes the family took trips to Mount Vernon and Arlington Cemetery. Many times he watched his father in political debate on the floor of the House of Representatives.

As a congressman's son, young Charles was in a position to watch history in the making. At first he was too young to comprehend the debates and speeches. He was aware, however, that President Theodore Roosevelt was an important person. Charles would always remember the sight of that dynamic man. His father served five terms in Congress, and with the passing years young Charles took an increasing interest in national and world affairs. He followed the Roosevelt-Taft disagreement, which split the Republican party and paved the way for the election of Democrat Woodrow Wilson as President in 1912. He heard the talk of impending war across the Atlantic in Europe.

In 1912, Charles Lindbergh saw his first airplane. With his mother, he had ridden over to Fort Myer, Virginia, to see one of the Wright Brothers' machines. It was a pusher-type biplane which resembled a kite more than a modern-day aircraft. The pilot sat out in front, completely exposed to the elements. "You could see the pilot clearly out front," Lindbergh would remember, "pants legs flapping, and cap visor pointed backward to streamline in the wind." The plane raced an automobile around an oval track in front of the grandstand while young Lindbergh cheered in wide-eyed excitement. From that moment, Charles Lindbergh was "fascinated with flying."

There was one other place in Washington, D.C., that attracted the congressman's son—the Smithsonian Institution. Even today, it remains one of the most exciting museums in America. But something has been added since Charles Lindbergh visited the place so many years ago. Today, there is a silver-colored airplane suspended from the ceiling which attracts as much interest as any exhibit in the Smithsonian. On the nose of the plane is painted the name, *Spirit of St. Louis.*

In this photo, young Charles is shown with his father, C. A. Lindbergh, a Republican Congressman who served in Washington for five terms.

In this 1908 photo, Wilbur and Orville Wright are shown with one of their early airplanes. Four years later Charles Lindbergh was taken to see his first airplane, one much like this one, which also belonged to the Wright Brothers.

Danger-A Challenge

Charles Lindbergh was a teen-ager when he began to develop a deep interest in mechanical things. The first machine he could call his own was a bicycle which he often took apart and reassembled. He was able to keep the farm equipment on the Lindbergh place in top working order.

He always enjoyed the times he spent in Detroit, where he stayed with his Grandfather Land. The doctor had laboratories in his basement and in several rooms of the house, where he made dental plates and conducted many scientific experiments. Dr. Land allowed his grandson to use many of the tools, machines, and instruments as he encouraged the scientific and mechanical aptitudes of the boy. Charles admired his grandfather. "He is as wise as he is old," he once wrote, "and he can make

anything with his hands." The doctor was, Charles reported, "always ready to answer my questions and teach me the use of his tools."

War had come to Europe and young Lindbergh followed with interest the accounts of air battles in the skies over the Western Front. He soon could recognize at a glance the various war planes produced by Germany, France, and England. He read with excitement the accounts of the war "aces"—pilots who had shot down at least five enemy planes.

Airplanes were very expensive, however, and the boy concentrated his interest in automobiles. In the summer of 1916, when he was only fourteen years old, Charles drove his mother and an uncle to California in the family car —a Saxon. In those days, of course, there were few good roads. In the West

As a high schooler, Charles Lindbergh thrived on danger. Here he speeds along a country road on his Excelsior motorcycle.

there were only wagon trails. The journey, which took five weeks, proved to be a real test of the boy's mechanical abilities. Time and again the car broke down, but young Charles was up to the task of making repairs. Eventually, the three arrived safely in Los Angeles.

In his last year of high school at Little Falls, Charles acquired an Excelsior motorcycle which provided him with a new mechanical challenge. It also whetted his appetite for danger. He drove his motorcycle at breakneck speed along the dirt roads, sometimes taking shortcuts through the woods or along the steep banks of the Mississippi. He seemed to thrive on danger and yet, much to the amazement of his friends, he never had an accident.

Danger to Charles Lindbergh was like a personal challenge. He made a sort of game of accepting personal risk just to prove a thing could be done. Yet he did not run risks in an unthinking or completely foolhardy manner. He carefully considered each problem and calculated the percentage of chance. He felt that with skill and intelligence, he could reduce the odds against success.

America had entered the war by the time Charles began his senior year in high school. A new government slogan was urging the farmers to produce to the maximum. "Food Will Win the War," it said, and Charles was excused from school from March until May to help on his father's farm. Once again he had a chance to prove his mechanical ability. His father had purchased a tractor—only the second one in Morrison County—which was delivered in pieces. Charles assembled the machine in three days. It ran perfectly.

In that early summer of 1918, Charles Lindbergh graduated from Little Falls High School and became a farmer. With characteristic devotion to a job, the young man worked hard. He persuaded his father to invest in more stock and soon the well-organized farm was bustling with cows, sheep, poultry, and hogs. More land was put to the plow and planted with a variety of crops. To supplement his farm income, young Charles acquired a milking-machine dealership. He also sold farm engines, and was thus able to work closely with machines and mechanical things.

With the end of World War I on November 11, 1918, the huge market for farm products began to decline.

Soon there was a great surplus of produce in America and prices started to tumble. The Lindberghs soon realized that farming was becoming an unprofitable business. Charles had not intended to remain a farmer all his life. His yen for adventure and excitement was too strong to permit him to devote his life to agriculture with its quiet daily routine. There was a spirit within him which craved travel, danger, and a profession associated with machines.

After talking things over with his parents, Charles decided to leave the farm and continue his education. In the fall of 1920, he found a tenant for the farm and enrolled as a freshman at the University of Wisconsin. He chose to major in mechanical engineering.

Charles lived with his mother in Madison, where she took a teaching job at Emerson Junior High School. His parents had been separated for many years. Charles had always made his home with his mother, though he spent much time with his father.

C.A. had continued to be active in politics and in the magazine publishing business. But from the time he had chosen not to run for re-election to the House of Representatives in 1916, C.A.'s political fortunes had dimmed. He was defeated for the Senate in 1916, lost in the Minnesota gubernatorial primary in 1918 and, in the same year Charles entered college, was badly defeated in yet another congressional election. Charles had accompanied his father during his election campaigns but never developed an active interest in politics.

In the iceboat he built when he was a student at the University of Wisconsin, Lindbergh satisfied his craving for danger by sailing over frozen lakes at incredible speeds.

The young man who entered college in the fall of 1920 was slender and light in weight, but in excellent physical condition after two hard years on the farm. He had already reached his full height of six feet three inches. He believed earnestly in physical fitness and for that reason never smoked or drank. Yet he did not participate in sports or athletics.

Charles was a shy young man and had acquired his father's trait of being a "loner." He made few friends and remained apart from his classmates. The one or two friends he did make in Madison shared with him the same love of machines. They, too, had motor-cycles. When the snow and ice made cycle riding too dangerous even for Lindbergh, he dismantled his motor and mounted it on an iceboat he had constructed. By fashioning an airplane propeller to the motor, he was able to skim over frozen Lake Mendota at tremendous speeds.

Lindbergh's extra-curricular activities also included swimming, hiking, and rifle shooting with the ROTC rifle team. In his only team association, Charles was easily the star marksman. Time and again he would score fifty consecutive bull's-eyes.

During his summer vacation of 1921, Charles attended an army field artillery school at Camp Knox, Kentucky (now Fort Knox). He returned to college in the fall without much enthusiasm. "The long hours of study at college were very trying for me," he would remember later. "I had spent most of my life out-

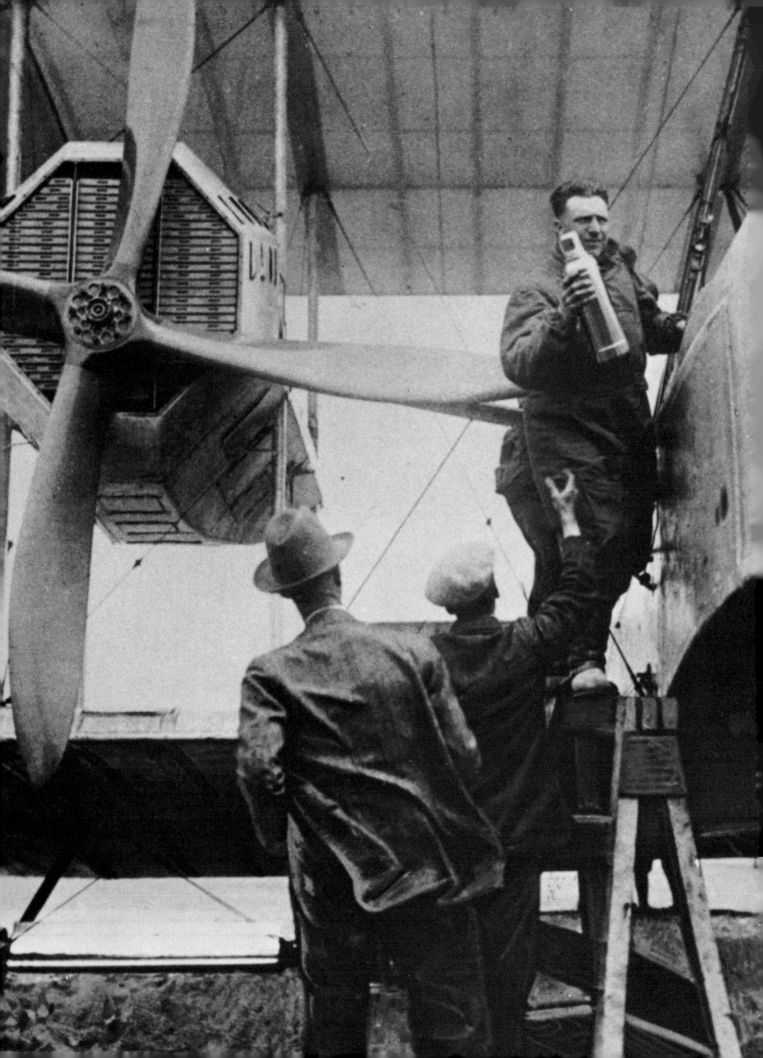

doors and had never found it necessary to spend more than a part of my time in study." Though his professors would claim he could do "A" work if he put his mind to it, Charles remained only an average student. He was restless. He needed a more active life.

His interest in aviation had increased during the previous two years. He had followed with excitement the exploits of Lieutenant Commander Albert C. Read and the flight of his American naval seaplane from Newfoundland to England by way of the Azores and Portugal in 1919. A little later, the flight of Alcock and Brown from Newfoundland to Ireland captured Lindbergh's imagination. After talking things over with his mother, who tried to dissuade him, Charles at last came to a decision:

"Soon after the start of my third semester at Wisconsin, I decided to study aeronautics in earnest, and if, after becoming better acquainted with the subject, it appeared to have a good future, I intended to take it up as a lifework. I remained at the University of Wisconsin long enough to finish the first half of my sophomore year."

At the end of March, 1922, Charles Lindbergh left college forever. Astride his Excelsior, he headed for Lincoln, Nebraska, and the Nebraska Aircraft Corporation. The corporation manufactured the Lincoln Standard, an open-cockpit, two-seater biplane. They also offered a course of flying instruction.

This journey, which began on a battered old Excelsior motorcycle, would culminate five years later in the lonely skies above the Atlantic Ocean. Charles Lindbergh's ride with destiny had begun.

Among the events that sharpened Charles Lindbergh's interest in aviation was the 1919 flight of Alcock and Brown from Newfoundland to England. Captain John Alcock, the pilot, is shown here placing food and provisions in the fuselage of his plane before takeoff for Europe.

Adventure-
A Vocation

Charles Lindbergh arrived at the Nebraska Aircraft Corporation factory on the first of April, 1922. It was a fascinating place for the air-minded young man who had never before been close enough to a plane to touch it. Wings were stacked in neat pairs waiting for assembly. Colorful fuselages lay on the floor of the shop. The smell of nitrate dope filled the air within the factory—a smell that would become a part of Lindbergh's life. The dope was used to treat and make taut the fabric covering of a plane. Charles was soon immersed in the work of building and assembling airplanes.

The fee for instruction at the flying "school" was five hundred dollars, which Charles paid in cash to Ray Page, president of the company. In return, he was to receive a specified number of flying hours under instruction. As it turned out, Charles was the only student. The school also had only one instructor, a hard-boiled former army pilot by the name of I. O. Biffle. "Biff,"

as the instructor was called, would not allow his student to fly during midday because of gusty winds. Lindbergh's flights were confined to the periods just after sunup and just before sunset.

The future Lone Eagle, who had immediately been dubbed "Slim," took his first airplane ride on April 9, 1922. The plane was a brand-new Lincoln Standard with a 150-horsepower Hispano-Suiza engine. Slim had watched with great interest as the plane was assembled that very morning. He was impressed with the infinite care with which the plane was put together.

Lindbergh then watched as the plane was taken aloft for a test flight. Assured that the plane functioned properly, the pilot, Otto Timm, landed and prepared to take up the plane's first passengers. Along with sixteen-year-old Harlan "Bud" Gurney, a worker at the factory, Lindbergh climbed into the front cockpit. It was Bud's first ride, too. With their leather helmets in place and goggles over their eyes, they waited with

In 1922, Lindbergh left college to go to the Nebraska Aircraft Corporation in Lincoln to take flying lessons. He is shown here on his arrival.

unconcealed excitement for Timm to start the plane. A mechanic pulled the propeller through at the call "contact" from Timm and the engine roared to life. Timm revved the engine, then nodded to the mechanics, who pulled the wheel chocks. The plane began to move.

Lindbergh has described his feeling on that first airplane ride: "The plane lurches forward . . . the tail rises as trees rush toward us . . . the ground recedes and we are resting on the air . . . Trees become bushes; barns, toys; cows turn into rabbits as we climb. I lose all conscious connection with the past. I live only in the moment in this strange, unmortal space, crowded with beauty, pierced with danger. The horizon retreats, and veils itself in haze. The great squared fields of Nebraska become a patchwork on a planet's disk."

Slim and Bud were both thrilled by their flight and grinned delightedly as they left the plane after landing. Both knew they had found their true calling. There was no longer any doubt as to the future of Charles Lindbergh.

By May, Slim had received a total of about eight hours of flight instruction and, according to Biff, was ready for his solo flight. But Ray Page would not allow such an inexperienced pilot to solo in an expensive airplane. He was pleased that Slim had proven to be such a good student, but unless the young man could post a bond to cover the plane in case of an accident, he couldn't trust the plane in his hands. Charles, though hurt and dismayed, could understand Ray's point of view. He would have to find a way to acquire more experience.

The plane in which Slim had trained was being sold to a pilot by the name of Erold Bahl, who was planning a barnstorming tour of southeastern Nebraska. The word "barnstorming" had been coined by groups of actors who often had to perform their plays in barns when touring rural areas. In aviation it meant flying to various small towns, landing in a convenient nearby field, and taking passengers for rides. To attract customers and crowds of watchers, the barnstormers would frequently perform eye-catching stunts. Slim asked Bahl if he could go along on the tour as mechanic and helper and even offered to pay his own expenses. Bahl agreed, and the pair left Lincoln late in May.

Slim proved to be a hard worker and an asset to the endeavor. He kept the plane clean, helped with the fueling, and even drummed up business in the crowds. Then one day he got the idea of climbing out on the lower wing of the plane as Bahl flew low over a small town. Onlookers gasped as they saw a lanky figure waving from the wing and pointing the way to the field where the plane would land. This death-defying stunt, with no parachute, drew the attention of the townspeople and business boomed. Bahl was so pleased he began paying Slim's expenses. The pair returned to Lincoln early in June after causing quite a sensation in southeastern Nebraska.

By now, Lindbergh's finances were getting rather low. He had a few hundred dollars deposited in a bank in Little Falls, but was determined to save this to put toward a plane of his own. To earn money, he took a job as handyman with the aircraft company. At this point in his life, Charles had achieved only part of his goal. He now could fly an airplane, but he still needed to solo and gain experience before he could make a living at flying. And his dream of owning a plane was yet to be realized.

On June 18, 1922, Lindbergh witnessed his first parachute jump. On that day a parachute maker by the name of Charles W. Harden demonstrated his

Lindbergh enters the cockpit for his first airplane ride on April 9, 1922. The plane was a brand-new Lincoln Standard with a 150-horsepower Hispano-Suiza engine.

product before a crowd that had gathered at the airport. Lindbergh was fascinated as Harden leaped from his plane 2000 feet above the field. Watching as the parachute blossomed, Lindbergh saw "a few gossamer yards grasping onto air and suspended below them, with invisible threads, a human life, a man who by stitches, cloth, and cord, had made himself a god of the sky for those immortal moments."

Harden landed safely, and as he gathered up his chute and walked away, Lindbergh knew he must try jumping from a plane. There was an instinctive fear at the thought of jumping into space at 2000 feet, but to Lindbergh the fear and the danger represented a personal challenge. It was a challenge he felt compelled to accept. Later he would explain: "The thought of crawling out onto the wing, through a hurricane of wind, clinging onto struts and wires hundreds of feet above the earth, and then giving up even that tenuous hold of safety and of substance, left in me a feeling of anticipation mixed with dread, of confidence restrained by caution, of courage salted through with fear . . . It was a love of the air and sky and flying, the lure of adventure, the appreciation of beauty. It lay beyond the descriptive words of men—where immortality is touched through with danger, where life meets death on equal plane; where man is more than man, and existence both supreme and valueless at the same instant."

Lindbergh approached Harden about the use of a parachute. The parachutist was surprised at the request, but was doubly surprised when Slim informed him that he wanted to make a "double jump." This involves jumping with two chutes. For the first part of the descent, the first chute is used. Then the first is cut away and the jumper falls freely once again until the second chute opens and carries him safely to the ground. Convinced that the young man was serious, Harden gave his consent. Then Slim spent the next three days persuading Ray Page to permit the jump. At last, in the early evening of a lovely June day, Lindbergh climbed into the front cockpit of a biplane and went aloft for his rendezvous with danger.

When the plane reached jump level, Lindbergh crawled out on the lower wing and attached his harness to the parachute hooks. Then, forcing fear from his mind with sheer willpower, he slipped gently off the wing where he dangled in space, 1800 feet above the ground. Now there was no turning back —the plane could not land with him in this position and he could not re-enter the plane. He *must* jump. He waited while the pilot gently maneuvered the plane to the exact spot over the airport. Then came the signal, and Slim yanked the bowknot that held the chutes in their canvas bag.

He was amazed to find that "all terror and sickening fear . . . stayed behind with the plane, as though they were too cowardly to make the final plunge." The first parachute blossomed soon after he pulled the bowknot. For a few moments he was suspended in silent space, drifting lazily through the evening sky. Then he cut loose the first chute and once again he was falling rapidly toward the ground below. He tumbled slowly as the earth rushed at him at an alarming rate. Why didn't

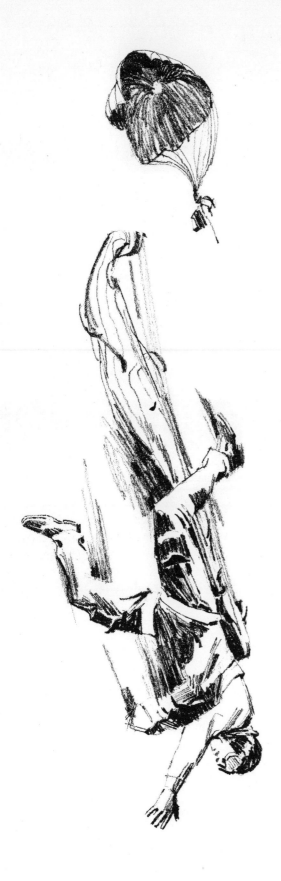

Lindbergh in the midst of his first double-parachute jump, a feat that was to mark the beginning of "Daredevil" Lindbergh's short career as a barnstormer.

———

the second chute open? Glancing over his shoulder, he saw the chute streaming behind him. At last, there was a "pop" as it filled with air and once again he was swinging lazily beneath the great white umbrella of muslin.

Below him, he could see the anxious, upturned faces of Ray Page, Bud Gurney, and Charles Harden. Realizing that he was going to miss the airport, Slim steered his chute as Harden had instructed, and landed safely on an adjacent golf course. The chute collapsed, and Lindbergh regained his feet as Page and the others rushed up to congratulate him. "Life changed after that jump," Slim would remember later. "I noticed it in the attitude of those who came to help gather up my chute—in Harden's acceptance of me as a brother parachutist, in Page's realization that I'd done what he didn't dare to do. I'd stepped suddenly to the highest level of daring—a level above even that which airplane pilots could attain."

With that challenge successfully met, Lindbergh turned once again to his dream—to become an experienced pilot and have a plane of his own. It would be some months yet before Slim could acquire the money to purchase an airplane. In the meantime, he would put to use his newfound skill as a wing walker and parachutist. For the next few months he would tour through the midwest on a barnstorming mission. Those who saw him would agree with the name printed boldly on colorful handbills which he scattered from a plane over small towns and villages. There are people in those towns today who still remember the performance of "Daredevil Lindbergh."

The Boy Barnstormer

In mid-July of 1922, Lindbergh accepted an offer to go on a barnstorming tour with "Banty" Rogers, who owned a Lincoln Standard. Rogers did not know how to fly, but he had hired a first-rate pilot by the name of H. J. "Cupid" Lynch. They had invited the twenty-year-old Lindbergh to go along as mechanic, general helper, and stunt man. After storing his motorcycle in the basement of the factory at Lincoln, Slim rode a train to Bird City, Kansas, to meet Rogers and Lynch.

For his first day on the job, "Daredevil Lindbergh" thrilled Rogers' hometown friends and neighbors with a parachute jump. Then the team took off on a tour that covered western Kansas, eastern Colorado, Montana, and Wyoming. Along the way, Slim learned the tricks of exhibition work. What seemed foolhardy and daredevil acts to the crowds on the ground had been carefully planned by Lindbergh. All possible safety factors had been

taken into account. Even the apparently suicidal stunt of standing on the top wing of a plane during a loop was, by his standards, quite safe. He had a special harness made which, when attached to fine but strong wire, eliminated all danger—he said.

A fourth member of the barnstorming team was a fox terrier named Booster. Booster, who belonged to Rogers, would rather fly than walk. He had no fear of altitude. For awhile he rode with Slim in the front cockpit of the plane, but later the men found a new way of carrying Booster. There was a "turtle-back" hump just behind the pilot's cockpit of the Lincoln Standard. The fliers attached a rubber mat to this hump and designed a special harness to hold Booster in place. The dog rode the plane as a cowboy rides a horse. It was a good thing he was harnessed on, however. From high altitudes he thought cows were rabbits and often tried to jump off and chase them. As Lindbergh

wrote later: "As far as animals were concerned, Booster never seemed able to relate altitude to size."

And so throughout the summer and early fall of 1922, the silver-colored Lincoln Standard, with Cupid Lynch at the controls, Daredevil Lindbergh walking on the wings, and Booster the flying dog "riding shotgun," startled and thrilled crowds from the Kansas plains to the Big Horn Mountains of Montana. In mid-October, as the first icy blasts of cold wind came moving down out of Canada, Lindbergh took leave of his companions and made his way southeastward, back to Nebraska. It hadn't been a particularly profitable tour in terms of money. But Slim had gained immeasurable experience in the world of flight. Lynch had allowed him to fly the plane at times and by now Slim was as much at home in the sky as he was on the ground.

"Science, freedom, beauty, adventure: what more could you ask of life?"

Lindbergh mused. "Aviation combined all the elements I loved. There was science in each curve of an airfoil, in each angle between strut and wire, in the gap of a spark plug, or the color of the exhaust flame. There was freedom in the unlimited horizon, on the open fields where one landed. A pilot was surrounded by beauty of earth and sky. He brushed treetops with the birds, leapt valleys and rivers, explored the cloud canyons he had gazed at as a child. Adventure lay in each puff of wind."

Lindbergh spent the winter of 1922-23 with his mother in Detroit, his father in Minneapolis, and even managed to get back for awhile to the farm in Little Falls. All the while he continued to dream of having a plane of his own. At the first hint of spring in Minnesota, he left for the sunny south and the realization of his dream. In April of 1923, at Souther Field in Georgia, he paid $500 for his first airplane.

The plane Slim had come to buy was a newly assembled surplus Jenny left over from World War I. He got a brand-new Curtiss OX-5 engine in the bargain, and a fresh coat of army olive-drab dope. It didn't look like much, even by 1923 standards, but Lindbergh was as proud of his Jenny as if it had been a sleek fighter plane.

The Jenny—officially the Curtiss JN-4D—was an open cockpit, two-seat biplane with a V-8 engine. It was never famed as a high-performance craft and had a cruising speed of only seventy-five miles per hour in calm air. The top wing, which was much longer than the lower, measured a little more than forty-three feet, and the space between the two wings was crisscrossed with struts, braces, and guy wires.

The Jenny was anything but a beauty queen. Her squarish, angular lines began with a blunt radiator at the nose and tapered gradually to where a rather fragile tail seemed to have been stuck on as an afterthought. If handled gently, the Jenny was a fairly stable airplane, and as such made an excellent trainer. It was the Model T of aviation and enjoyed the same affection and devotion of pilots that Henry Ford's "Tin Lizzie" did of automobile drivers.

In those days, no license was required to pilot an airplane. After Lindbergh had paid for the Jenny, a mechanic rolled it out on the line and pulled the prop through to start the engine. He was on his own—no questions asked. It had been some months since he had been at the controls of an airplane; and the Jenny did not respond like the Lincoln Standard. As a result, Lindbergh very nearly ended his flying career on his first attempt to solo. He intended to simply lift the plane off the ground

a few feet on the first couple of tries to get the "feel" of the Jenny.

Years later he would write of the incident: "I headed directly into the wind and opened the throttle—cautiously. The Jenny swerved a little. I kicked the opposite rudder. It swerved the other way. I straightened out—opened the throttle more—The tail lifted up—a bit too high—I pulled back on the stick—the tail skid touched—I pushed forward —pulled back—Before I knew it, I was in the air!—I cut the throttle—dropped too fast—opened it wide—ballooned up, right wing low—closed the throttle— yanked back on the stick—bounced down on wheel and wing skid."

Back safely on the ground, Lindbergh rolled to a stop in the middle of the airfield. It had been a close call—if the right wing had touched the ground a little harder, the Jenny might have cartwheeled itself into splinters. As it was, Lindbergh was more embarrassed than frightened. He couldn't decide if it had been a gust of wind that caused the plane to go wrong or simply bad flying. He decided to wait until evening when the air would be calm.

As he cut the engine of the Jenny, a stranger who introduced himself as Henderson sauntered up with a grin. "Why don't you let me jump in the front cockpit before you try that again?"

Lindbergh stammered an embarrassed explanation for his showing and then accepted Henderson's offer. An experienced pilot, Henderson was waiting for a newly purchased plane to be assembled. Once in the front cockpit, he signaled Slim to go ahead. It proved to be a lot easier with an instructor there to correct any serious errors. Lindbergh made a half-dozen smooth takeoffs and landings. Then he taxied the plane back to

---

This Jenny, a Curtiss JN-4D, is just like Charles Lindbergh's first airplane, which he bought for $500 in April of 1923. It was an open-cockpit, two-seat biplane that had been left over from World War I.

the line, thanked Henderson for his help, and waited for evening and calm air.

About five o'clock, Slim came back to the airfield and started the engine. As the sun set slowly over the forests and fields of rural Georgia, he flew alone for the first time. At last, at long last, he was by himself—high in a seemingly limitless sky, grinning exultantly over the edge of the cockpit at the earthlings below. He was now a member of a select group, a rare breed of man who leave their fellow human beings behind to find beauty and adventure in space. He celebrated this moment alone in his flimsy little Jenny. There would be other moments alone, moments that would stretch into historic hours for this young man who now came gliding back to earth in Georgia. But this was the first.

Slim spent another week at Souther Field practicing takeoffs and landings and learning the limitations and characteristics of the Jenny. By the end of the week, he had accumulated more than five hours of solo time, and he now felt experienced enough to head home for Minnesota. He was running low on cash, however, so he decided to do a little barnstorming to help defray his expenses. He set his course westward toward Texas and what was reputed to be good barnstorming country.

He made it to Meridian, Mississippi, the first day. The following morning he climbed slowly into a threatening sky and headed west again. With no compass and a rather poor map, Slim was

soon lost. Because there were storm clouds in the area, he decided to land in a field and find out exactly where he was. The landing was a smooth one, but in taxiing toward the shelter of a pine grove, Slim ran into a hidden ditch. The Jenny stood on its nose and threatened to go all the way over, but then settled back to a forty-five degree angle. Slim got out to survey the damage, which proved to be only a broken propeller. Nearby farmers came running to help, and together they righted the Jenny and pushed it to the pine grove. Slim then rode to the nearby town of Maben, Mississippi, with a storekeeper, and wired Souther Field for a new propeller.

Three days later the new prop arrived, and a large crowd gathered to watch Slim repair his plane and test it. Following a test flight, Slim announced he was ready to take up passengers. After considerable persuasion, a farmer stepped forward to become Lindbergh's first passenger. By the end of the day, he had made enough money to pay for the new propeller, his hotel bill, gasoline, and had made a little profit besides. At last young Charles Lindbergh was earning money in aviation.

Slim stayed in Maben two weeks, and during that time "hopped" some sixty passengers. One old lady asked him how much he would charge to take her up to heaven and leave her there. Most of his passengers, though, were happy to take their first airplane ride and return

During a short barnstorming tour in his new Jenny, Lindbergh taxied the plane into a ditch. The plane tipped up on its nose, which broke the propeller.

safely to earth where they would be acclaimed for their daring.

Slim headed west once more—this time with a compass installed in the plane. Across Louisiana and Arkansas to Texas he barnstormed. Sometimes he slept in a hammock between the wings of the Jenny after landing in some remote pasture. At last he turned northward and headed across Oklahoma and Kansas toward Lincoln, Nebraska, where there would be a grand reunion with his old friends at the factory.

Slim Lindbergh was now an accepted member of that carefree fraternity of men known as barnstormers, or "Gypsy Fliers." Nomads of the sky, they came and went, unattached and fancy free. In 1923, "bird men" were still a small, select group but wherever they landed, they met others with whom they shared a common experience. Earthlings were excluded from the little groups who sat around airfields "ground flying." With their planes securely tied down for the night, these few who found adventure in the sky would swap yarns about their flying experiences.

Charles Lindbergh was now twenty-one years old and a proven, if not experienced, pilot. He owned his own airplane. He had reached his goal. What now? Before that summer of 1923 was over, Charles Lindbergh was to set his sights on the next step of his flying career. His new goal was to become a commissioned officer in the United States Army Air Service Reserve.

Across the Country in a Canuck

In June of 1923, C. A. Lindbergh was running in the Minnesota primary election for the United States Senate. Though C.A. had never been up in a plane, he and his son decided that a speaking tour by air would lend a dramatic touch to his election campaign. As it turned out, the plan was short-lived. On the third "hop" of the tour, there was an accident. Though father and son escaped serious injury, the plane was out of commission for awhile once again. C.A. continued his campaign on the ground, but was badly beaten on election day.

For the remainder of the summer, Slim barnstormed through Minnesota, northern Iowa, and western Wisconsin. For one ten-day period, his adventurous mother flew with him. From the time of her first ride with her son, she had been a staunch flying enthusiast.

It was during this barnstorming tour that Slim first heard about the Army Air Service training program. A former graduate of the school advised him to apply for enrollment and Slim wrote immediately for the necessary forms. "I had always wanted to fly modern and powerful planes," he said. "The army offered the only opportunity."

There was, however, a more serious reason behind Lindbergh's goal. He was convinced that commercial aviation would one day become a significant industry in America. As the industry grew, so would the demand for experienced pilots. Lindbergh felt he could acquire experience and technical proficiency in the army. And, too, he would be getting paid while he learned.

In the meantime, Slim continued to barnstorm around the midwest and, in October, flew to St. Louis to attend

During C. A. Lindbergh's 1923 political campaign, Charles flew his father around Minnesota in the Jenny. On their third hop a crash occurred that put the plane out of commission, though neither father nor son was hurt.

the International Air Races at Lambert Field. He watched with excitement as Lieutenant A. J. Williams, USN, set a new world's speed record of 243.67 miles per hour. He also met his pal Bud Gurney and agreed to take him up for a double-parachute jump. Gurney had bad luck, however, and broke his arm as he landed on the edge of a ditch beside the field. His was the only injury of the entire meet.

After the races had ended, Lindbergh sold his Jenny. He made a fine profit on the deal, and it led to his first role as an instructor. The Iowan who bought the plane did not know how to fly and Slim included flying lessons in the transaction. Lindbergh also took on a second student who had purchased a plane.

In January, as requested, he reported to Chanute Field to take his entrance examinations, which he passed with flying colors. He would get his chance to become an army pilot.

While waiting for final orders to report for training, Slim went in search of adventure with a friend named Leon Klink who owned a Canuck OX-5. The Canuck was nothing more than a Canadian version of the Jenny. On a cold January day in 1924, the two young men jumped into the open cockpits of the plane and headed south from St. Louis toward warmer weather. After a stop at Perryville, Missouri, they flew to Kentucky, then to Tennessee, Mississippi, and Alabama. Along the way they "hopped" passengers to meet expenses before continuing on.

At Pensacola, Florida, where they had landed at the Naval Air Station, Slim had an accident with the Canuck. Taking the plane up for a test hop one morning, he suffered a loss of power soon after takeoff. He wheeled the plane back toward the field but he was too low and could not make it. Instead he caromed off a sand hill, which smashed his landing gear and put a wheel through his lower wing. Then the plane plowed into another hill and came to a stop with its propeller smashed. Slim was unhurt and the navy lent assist-

Lindbergh examines a new propeller on a friend's Canuck OX-5. The plane had been damaged when Lindbergh landed the airplane in a rough field.

ance with repairs to the Canuck. Within a week they were on their way west.

One evening, over western Texas, Lindbergh landed the plane in the town square of a place called Camp Wood. The takeoff from the town was going to be pretty tricky. Slim intended to use one of the streets as a runway despite the fact that he would have only two feet to spare as he roared between a pair of telephone poles. He almost made it. There was a rough spot in the street, however, just fifty feet from where the plane would pass between the poles. This little rut jarred the Canuck a fraction off course and, before Slim could correct it, the right wing tip hit a pole. He had missed by three inches! The impact swung the plane around and it crashed headlong into a hardware store, sending pots, pans, pitchforks, and paint cans flying all over the store.

Slim was unhurt and later described the incident with a grin. "The merchant thought an earthquake was in progress and came running out into the street. He was highly pleased to find an airplane halfway into his place of business and not only refused to accept anything for damages, but would not even allow us to have the wall repaired. He said the advertising value was much more than the destruction."

In a few days, with a new propeller and some patchwork on the fabric, the pair of intrepid fliers were again on their way to California. They never made it. Two nights later they landed near Maxon, Texas, in an area covered with cactus and Spanish dagger. A takeoff attempt failed the next morning as these sharp-edged plants ripped through the fabric of wings and fuselage. At least this time the propeller was undamaged.

Klink hopped a passing freight train to El Paso and returned with fabric, glue, string, and nails. Borrowing an ax, a butcher knife, and a needle and thread, the two men soon had the plane in shape to fly. Klink, though, decided to ride a train to California while Slim flew the Canuck to Brooks Field, Texas, for his enlistment in the army.

Lindbergh landed his battered, scarecrow of a plane at Brooks Field on the day he was due. Army fliers and mechanics came out to gaze in amazement at the beat-up old crate of an airplane now parked on their immaculate field. Huge chunks of fabric were missing and the skeleton framework was showing through. A splice-brace, wound with cord, supported one wing like a broken arm in a sling. One tire was nearly flat and the other missing entirely. The commanding officer of the base issued a plain and explicit order— "Get that *thing* out of here!"

Obligingly, Lindbergh hopped the weary old bird over to a nearby commercial field in San Antonio. Four days later, on March 19, 1924, he was enlisted as a Flying Cadet in the army.

This day marked a turning point in the life of Charles Lindbergh. All his past flying experience had been for fun and adventure. Now however, the exciting days of barnstorming, wing walking, and roaming aimlessly around the country were past. Henceforth, his flying would be technical and scientific. More and more he would become concerned with aviation as an industry. Commercial aviation would demand higher standards of safety, flying ability, engineering, and instrumentation. The research, development, and testing of new aircraft, new instruments, and navigational aids would require sober, dedicated, technical-minded pilots capable of more than "seat-of-your-pants" flying.

The future of commercial aviation would require something beyond technical ability and scientific knowledge, however. It would need courage and daring, carefully considered and applied. It would need dedicated men who could calculate the odds, take the next measured step into the unknown, and return with knowledge. Charles Lindbergh possessed the courage and daring. He set out now to acquire the technical skill to balance these traits.

From Army to Airmail

For the first time in his life, Charles devoted all his energies to his schoolwork—willingly. Here at Brooks, every subject he touched on received his full interest and devotion. Ground school classes in aerodynamics, celestial navigation, machine guns, power plants, radio theory, military law, and many other subjects demanded long hours of study. In later years, Lindbergh explained his attitude at Brooks:

"Before, I'd always gone to school because I had to go, because it was considered the proper thing to do. Here, I was going to school because I wanted to learn, to complete the course, to gain my Air Service bars and wings. I studied after classes, through the weekends, often far into the night. At times I slipped into my bunk with swimming head, but I had the satisfaction of watching my grade average climb slowly through the 80's and into the 90's."

Lindbergh and six other cadets were assigned to a master sergeant named Winston for flight training. Slim came to admire Winston as one of the finest pilots at Brooks. The training planes used for primary training were Jennies and, of course, Lindbergh felt at home in the cockpit. There were two big differences between these Jennies and his old plane, however. These planes had the throttle on the left side of the cockpit, which meant the pilot had to fly with his right hand on the control stick. The other feature of the army Jenny was a more-powerful engine. Slim's old OX-5, 90-horsepower motor had often been barely powerful enough to sustain flight. These Army planes had 150-horsepower Hispano-Suizas, which considerably improved the performance of the Jenny.

During these early weeks at Brooks, Lindbergh's life was struck with a deep personal tragedy. In April he received a telegram informing him that his father was very ill and probably would not live long. Grief-stricken, Slim requested and received a short furlough and hastened to Minnesota to bid good-bye to his dying father. After a few quiet hours at his father's bedside, the saddened

A few weeks after Lindbergh had enlisted in the Army, he was called home to see his father, who was dying in a hospital in Minnesota.

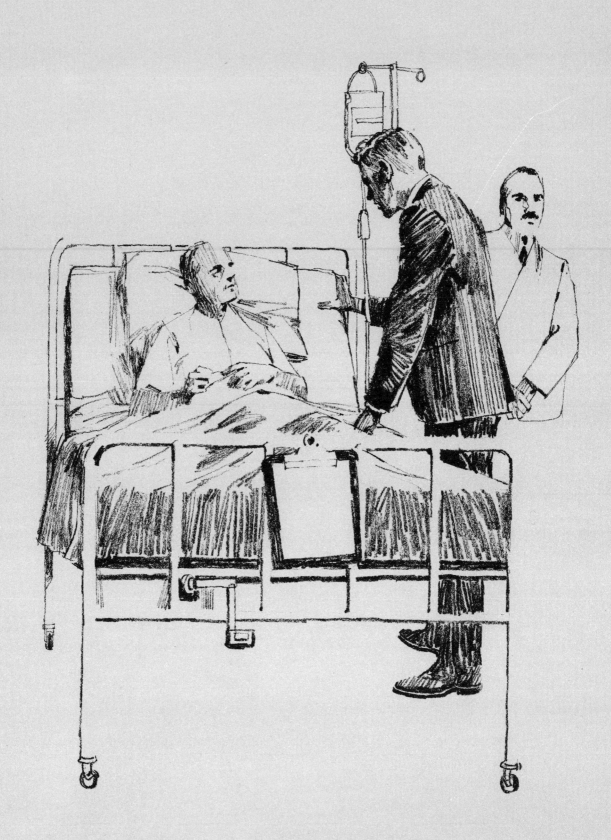

young man returned to his flight school in Texas. A month later on May 24, 1924, C. A. Lindbergh died in a hospital at Crookston, Minnesota.

Back at Brooks Field, Lindbergh immersed himself even more deeply in his studies in an effort to forget the pain of personal tragedy. The weeks slipped by quickly, and soon it was September. The long hot Texas summer was over. Around the country, talk centered on the presidential race between President Calvin Coolidge and his Democratic opponent, John Davis. Sports fans were watching Babe Ruth and the New York Yankees try to capture the American League pennant for the second year in a row. But in Texas, Charles Lindbergh was concerned about his final examinations in primary flight training. When the results were announced, Lindbergh had finished second in his class and, along with thirty-two others, was transferred to Kelly Field for advanced training. At last he would be able to fly the powerful planes he had dreamed of.

At Kelly, students were given their basic training in De Haviland biplanes with 400-horsepower Liberty engines. This was a considerable improvement over the Jenny, but even the "DH" had its limitations. Loops and spins were prohibited in the DH, which had a bad habit of shedding its wings in high-speed dives. The plane had the somber nickname of "Flaming Coffin" because of its tendency to burst into flames on a crash landing. Charles soon had the "feel" of the DH, however, and looked forward to flying faster and stronger aircraft.

The DH was a two-place airplane. On cross-country training flights one cadet would pilot the plane while another acted as observer. For the return flight, they would exchange seats. During gunnery practice, the pilot fired the Browning machine guns, which were aimed straight ahead and were synchronized to fire through the propeller. The rear-seat observer had twin Lewis machine guns which could be pointed in any direction.

After completing the gunnery course in the De Havilands, the cadets were given their choice of the type of airplane in which they would like to specialize. Slim chose the pursuit branch. He was soon flying the speedy little S.E.5 Scout. He chose this branch because "pursuit combines a little of every branch of the air corps. In addition to formation combat, dog fighting, and ground strafing, the pursuit pilot is often called upon to make observations and do light bombing." Today the word "pursuit" has been changed to "fighter."

This branch of the air corps satisfied Lindbergh's craving for danger. He delighted in the tight formation flying

where often there was less than ten feet between wing tips as the planes power-dived for thousands of feet. At last he had at his beck and call an airplane that would dance across the sky. He thrilled at the way the S.E.5 responded to his touch, twisting through Immelmann turns, shrieking earthward in vertical dives, and tiptoeing scant inches above the tops of trees. This was real flying.

On March 15, 1925, 18 of the original 104 cadets graduated at Kelly Field. By the end of the course, Lindbergh was the most accomplished flier of the group. He finished first in the class with a grade average of 93. The class celebrated with a farewell dinner in San Antonio. Most of the newly commissioned officers resigned immediately from active service and became members of the Air Service Reserve Corps. Second Lieutenant Charles A. Lindbergh was among them.

He had made many good friends among the pilots in St. Louis, so Slim decided to go back there. He headed north from Texas by train. At least there would be some sort of work available in St. Louis while he searched and waited for an opening in the field of commercial aviation.

Soon after his arrival, Slim was contacted by William and Frank Robertson, two brothers who owned and operated the Robertson Aircraft Corpora-tion. They were bidding for a govern-ment contract to fly airmail between St. Louis and Chicago. They offered Lindbergh the position of chief pilot for the enterprise, providing their bid was successful. Slim agreed but, as it would be some months before the contract was awarded, he needed other work in the meantime. For awhile he barnstormed around Missouri and Illinois and also found some students to instruct.

The months passed quickly in 1925. Slim kept busy barnstorming for the "Mil-Hi Airways and Flying Circus" in Colorado. He also spent two weeks of active army duty at Richards Field in Missouri, and joined the One Hundred and Tenth Observation Squadron of the Missouri National Guard. Here he was promoted to first lieutenant and later to captain.

In the fall of 1925, military aviation became headline news as Colonel Billy Mitchell faced a court-martial for voic-ing views that the military high com-mand was negligent in its administra-tion of national defense. Mitchell be-lieved in air power and insisted that battleships and other large vessels were vulnerable to air attack. Proof of his views would come in the disaster at Pearl Harbor in 1941. But in 1925, Billy Mitchell was found guilty of conduct prejudicial to good order and military discipline, and was suspended from the

service for five years. Army pilots like Charles Lindbergh, however, never lost their faith in air power as a major factor in modern warfare.

Early in 1926, the Robertson Aircraft Corporation won its airmail contract and Lindbergh immediately took the job of chief pilot. He was authorized to find and hire two more pilots for the Chicago-St. Louis run, and he chose two ex-army buddies, Philip R. "Red" Love and Thomas P. "Nellie" Nelson. Next, he flew the route to be used and selected nine landing fields, which the government leased for the service.

On the fifteenth of April, 1926, Lindbergh took off from Maywood Field, Chicago, on the inaugural flight of the Robertson airmail operation. The plane he flew was one of the company's fourteen-year-old, rebuilt army De Havilands—the "Flaming Coffins" he had flown at Kelly Field. The front cockpit had been converted to a mail compartment and the pilot now flew from the rear seat. It was something of a shoestring operation financially, and the company just could not afford to buy newer, more-efficient aircraft.

At last Charles Lindbergh had a job in commercial aviation. It was a demanding job that required a pilot with exceptional flying ability. Schedules had to be maintained despite inclement weather. Pilots took pride in being punctual with their mail deliveries. The haphazard itinerary of the barnstormer was a thing of the past. Airmail flying was not routine, however, as Lindbergh would discover in the months to come. The challenge of danger and the sense of adventure were part of every flight.

Before the year 1926 had ended, however, Charles Lindbergh would be preparing to accept the greatest challenge in the young history of aviation. From that April inaugural flight only thirteen months would elapse before he would face the challenge of transatlantic flight.

At the climax of his fight for air power, Colonel Billy Mitchell (standing left) was court-martialed in 1925 for voicing his views publicly. Neither he nor Army pilots like Charles Lindbergh, however, ever lost their faith in air power as a major factor in modern warfare.

One March day in 1925, a flight of nine SE-5 pursuit planes cruised the skies above Kelly Field, Texas, searching for "enemy" planes. One three-plane unit was comprised of Cadet Love, leading; Lieutenant McAllister, flying right wing; and Cadet Lindbergh, flying left wing. Sighting an "enemy" several hundred feet below (an Army DH4B), the formation commander signaled for an "attack." Cadet Lindbergh nosed his SE-5 over and roared down for a close pass at the DH. Shrieking past the slower plane, Lindbergh pulled back on his control stick and zoomed up in a left climbing turn. Suddenly he felt a jolt and then a crash which seemed to halt his plane in midair.

Unhurt by the impact, he glanced around to find what had happened. Just a few feet away sat Lieutenant McAllister in the seat of his SE-5, which was locked together with Lindbergh's plane. The pilots stared at each other in amazement for a moment and then the planes started falling through the air in a death plunge toward the ground 5000 feet below. Both men immediately climbed out of their cockpits and leaped away from the falling SE-5's. Their parachutes billowed and the planes hurtled past them, still locked together, to crash in a field and burst into flames. Lindbergh and McAllister both landed safely to become members number twelve and thirteen of the "Caterpillar Club." This club was an informal group of men who had in common the fact that their lives had been saved by emergency parachute jumps. Parachutes in those days were made of silk, which comes from the silkworm caterpillar. This was where the club got its unusual name.

The most significant aspect of this near tragedy, however, lay in the fact that Charles Lindbergh, who landed before McAllister, became the first man in history to survive a midair collision of airplanes.

ROBERTSON
AIRCRAFT CORPORATION
RAC

Birth of a Spirit

"Neither snow, nor rain, nor heat, nor gloom of night stays these couriers from the swift completion of their appointed rounds." These words of Herodotus and the byword of postmen became the creed of Charles Lindbergh and the airmail pilots of Robertson's Aircraft Corporation. In foul weather or fair, flying clumsy De Havilands in and out of unlighted airfields, with no radio communication between ground and plane, these skilled and daring airmen did their best to meet their schedules. During the first five months of operation, the company pilots made their connections on more than ninety-eight per cent of their trips.

By September, however, the weather started to turn bad, and things began to go wrong. On the night of September 16, 1926, Slim took off from a field at Peoria, Illinois, headed for Chicago. The

---

In 1926 Charles Lindbergh was chief airmail pilot for the Robertson Aircraft Corporation of St. Louis. Here he sits in the cockpit of one of the company's clumsy De Haviland airplanes prior to a takeoff.

sky was almost clear of clouds but, part-way to Maywood Field, a dense, low fog moved under Lindbergh's wings. After nearly three hours of vain searching for a hole in the fog, Slim ran out of gas and had to abandon the plane at 5000 feet. He landed within two miles of where the plane had crashed, and a farmer drove him to the wrecked DH. The mail proved to be undamaged, and was soon on its way by train.

Two months later, in November, he had to "bail out" again—this time into the teeth of a raging blizzard at an altitude of 13,000 feet. He landed safely by parachute near the town of Covell, Illinois, but was unable to locate the plane. Leaving his parachute at a farmhouse, he caught a train to Chicago and early the next morning flew back to Covell in clear weather. He spotted the wrecked plane from the air, only 500 feet behind the house where he had left his parachute. Again, the mail was undamaged.

Of course, the weather was not always bad and on many warm summer nights, Lindbergh enjoyed the solitude and sense of freedom he experienced on these mail flights. One night, in September of 1926, on a flight to Chicago, he began to think about the recent crash of the Sikorsky Tri-motor, flown by the French war-ace Rene Fonck. Fonck and three other men had attempted to take off from Roosevelt Field, Long Island, in quest of the Orteig prize. The plane, overburdened with 2380 gallons of gasoline, had been unable to lift off the ground, even with the concentrated power of its three engines. Fonck and his co-pilot survived the crash, but the other two men burned to death. As he floated high above the earth in his DH, Slim began to ponder the problems involved in a transatlantic flight.

"For one thing," he decided, "a plane that's got to break the world's record for nonstop flying should be stripped of every excess ounce of weight." He made a mental list of items such a flight could do without—radios, hot food, all but the minimum survival equipment. And for that matter, he believed, "It certainly doesn't take four men to fly a plane across the ocean."

Giving the subject more thought as he cruised along over Illinois, Slim decided that by cutting the crew to only two men, a plane could carry some three or four hundred more pounds of gasoline. This would be a big safety factor in itself. "If it were me," Slim mused, "I'd trade the navigator for extra gasoline, too, and make the flight alone. And I'd use a single-engine plane which would present less head resistance and, consequently, give a greater cruising range. I'm sure I could!"

The thought of making the flight himself excited Slim's imagination. "Why shouldn't I fly from New York to Paris? I'm almost twenty-five. I have more than four years of aviation behind me, and close to two thousand hours in the air. I've barnstormed over half of the forty-eight states. I've flown my mail through the worst of nights. I'm a captain in the One Hundred and Tenth Observation Squadron of Missouri's National Guard. Why am I not qualified for such a flight?"

By the time Slim landed that night at Maywood Field, he was convinced that he could make the flight successfully. Here was the greatest challenge of his life. Here was adventure beyond any he had ever dreamed of before. He knew he *must* make the flight—the challenge and the danger were irresistible.

Such a flight would take considerable financial backing. Lindbergh had only about $2000 to put into such a venture, and a plane capable of such a flight would cost many times that. He decided to approach some St. Louis businessmen for the backing he would need. The next few months he devoted to "selling" his idea to potential backers.

At last he had several aviation-minded and public-spirited men who

---

The illustration shows Lindbergh as he spots the wreckage of a mail plane from which he had bailed out during a raging blizzard the day before.

would invest in the enterprise. They were Major A. B. Lambert, an aviation pioneer for whom the St. Louis airfield was named; J. D. Wooster Lambert; Earl Thompson, an insurance executive; the Robertson brothers; Harry H. Knight, a broker, and his father Harry F. Knight; Harold Bixby, a banker; and E. Lansing Ray, a newspaperman. Together with Slim's money, the organization had pledged a total of $15,000 with which to buy a plane and pay for other expenses related to the flight. At Bixby's suggestion, they decided to name the plane *Spirit of St. Louis*.

Lindbergh was to choose the type of airplane that would be used. He was particularly interested in a Bellanca monoplane with a Wright Whirlwind engine. Negotiations to buy the plane failed, however, and he tried one or two other companies. Fokker wanted about $90,000 for a plane especially designed for such a trip. A Sikorsky such as Fonck had used cost more than $30,000. Slim was in despair when a telegram arrived from a little-known company in San Diego, called Ryan Airlines. They would build a plane capable of making the flight for about $6000 without motor and instruments. Slim immediately caught a train for San Diego.

The Ryan factory was a dilapidated building not far from the waterfront on San Diego's beautiful bay. The smell of dead fish from nearby canneries mingled with the odor of aircraft dope. There was little activity in the factory, which employed fewer than a dozen men. But the key men, including president B. F. Mahoney and chief engineer Donald Hall, were young, eager men anxious to do business. After a day of preliminary discussions, Lindbergh wired to the organization at St. Louis that Ryan would build the plane, complete with Whirlwind J-5 engine and standard instru-

ments, for $10,580. On February 25, 1927, the approval to go ahead came back and work was begun on the *Spirit of St. Louis*.

The plane was a modified Ryan M-2 fuselage with an enlarged wingspan of 46 feet and an overall length of 27 feet 8 inches. In its final configuration, the M-2 became the model "NYP" (New York-Paris). It carried fuel tanks in the main fuselage, the nose, and had three wing tanks, for a total capacity of 425 gallons. The 8 foot 9 inch propeller was turned by the 223 BHP Wright J-5C engine. Flight tests proved the plane to have a maximum air speed at sea level of 129 miles per hour.

The Ryan factory workers were soon caught up in Lindbergh's enthusiasm and every man put his complete energies into the task of building the plane. While they worked, Slim pored over navigation charts as he plotted the course he would follow over the Atlantic.

The quest for the Orteig prize became a race now. Commander Richard E. Byrd was nearly ready to make the attempt in a Fokker Tri-motor, the *America*. Lieutenant Commander Noel Davis was testing his keystone Pathfinder plane, the *American Legion*, also a three-engine craft. The Wright-Bellanca, which Lindbergh had hoped to buy, was now named the *Columbia* and was being readied for the flight. In France, Charles Nungesser and François Coli, two war heroes, were nearly ready to fly from Paris to New York in their single-engine biplane, the *White Bird*. Time was of the essence now, and Lindbergh and the Ryan people worked hard to complete the *Spirit of St. Louis*.

At last, on the twenty-eighth of April, the plane was ready. Taken to an airfield at Dutch Flats in sections, it had been assembled and was now ready for a test flight. Lindbergh was delighted

Some of the pilots who tried unsuccessfully to win the Orteig Prize are shown here. Clockwise from center: Commander Richard E. Byrd, Lieutenant Commander Noel Davis, Captain Charles Nungesser, Clarence Chamberlin, and Lieutenant François Coli.

with the performance of the plane and found only one or two minor irregularities. At last, on May 10, the tests were completed and Slim left San Diego on his transcontinental flight to New York. Fourteen hours and twenty-five minutes later, after diving across Lambert Field at 160 miles per hour, Lindbergh touched down in St. Louis. The following morning he pointed the *Spirit of St. Louis* toward the rising sun and New York City. Seven hours later he landed at Curtiss Field, Long Island, having cracked the transcontinental flight record by more than five hours.

By now there were only two other planes actively in the race for the Orteig prize. On May 8, Nungesser and Coli had left Paris. They were never heard from again. On April 26, the *American Legion* had crashed at Langley Field, Virginia, killing Noel Davis and his co-pilot. On April 16, the *America* had crashed at Teterboro, New Jersey, injuring three of the four-man crew.

The *America* had been repaired and was now poised on nearby Roosevelt Field for the transatlantic flight. In another hangar on Curtiss Field, the *Columbia* was undergoing last-minute mechanical checks before taking off for Paris with Clarence Chamberlin at the controls and his financial backer, Charles Levine, accompanying him. By now the country and the world were following the news of these preparations and most were rooting for the underdog —Slim Lindbergh.

At least he seemed to be the underdog. The other groups were lavishly equipped with large and expensive aircraft, numerous mechanics, and support personnel. Lindbergh was all by himself with limited funds and a little silver-colored airplane that was dwarfed by Byrd's huge Fokker. "Lucky Lindy" they dubbed him—the "Flyin' Fool."

Lucky he may have been, but Charles Lindbergh was anything but a fool. He did not count on luck for success. All contingencies had been carefully considered and he approached the trial with a confidence born of knowledge and skill, balanced with cool daring and personal courage. He had arrived at his moment of destiny.

On his way to New York from San Diego in the Spirit of St. Louis, *Lindbergh lands at Lambert Field in St. Louis for an overnight stop.*

59

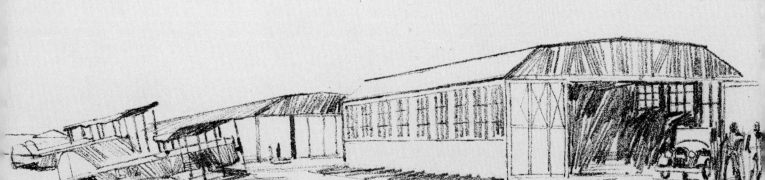

New York to Paris

I'm in the air with full tanks and a following wind!" Lindbergh was exultant as he cruised out over Long Island Sound and headed for Paris. "The engine has withstood its test of power. It's throttled down, turning smoothly and easily. The *Spirit of St. Louis* is no longer an unruly mechanical device, as it was during takeoff; it's no longer balanced on a pinpoint; rather, it seems to form an extension of my own body, ready to follow my wish as the hand follows the mind's desire—instinctively, without commanding."

By now the word had been flashed by radio to the world that the quiet, shy young American was on his way. As he cruised very low over New England, people gathered in the streets and on the rooftops along his flight path to catch a glimpse of his plane. All America, it seemed, listened for flash radio bulletins and followed his progress on maps and atlases. In Detroit, his mother, who had made a quick trip to New York to wish him luck, told reporters that the next day would be either the happiest or saddest of her life.

On the morning of May 20, 1927, a small crowd of people gathered at Roosevelt Field, Long Island, to watch Charles Augustus Lindbergh take off on his solo flight to Paris in the Spirit of St. Louis.

By the end of the second hour, the *Spirit of St. Louis* had passed over the Massachusetts coast south of Boston and had disappeared over the ocean. This was Slim's first real test of navigation. For more than two hours he was out of sight of land. He passed the test beautifully. When the Nova Scotia coast appeared on the horizon, he was only six miles from his planned landfall.

Onward he flew, over Nova Scotia and Cape Breton Island and then northeast over open water toward Newfoundland. He followed the Burin Peninsula and then crossed over Placentia Bay where, fourteen years later, President Roosevelt and Prime Minister Churchill would meet to draft a document called the Atlantic Charter.

After climbing to cross the Avalon Peninsula, he dove down again to pass low over the city of Saint John's. This had meant a slight detour from his planned route, but Lindbergh explained later: "Suppose I'd had a forced landing on the ocean. There'd be an advantage in people knowing that I went down somewhere east of Saint John's. No one would waste time searching for me along the coast as they searched for Nungesser and Coli." Men and women looked up as he roared over the city and across the harbor with its fleet of fishing boats. And then it was gone. In a few moments North America had slipped behind. Now the scene was one of vast emptiness—a great expanse of Atlantic Ocean, scattered clouds in a darkening sky and a lone monoplane winging eastward. Ahead lay Ireland—2000 miles away.

From that point, the flight became one of tedium and an increasingly difficult battle against fatigue and sleep. There were moments of danger, but danger served as an antidote to sleepiness. "When it's imminent and real, it cuts like a rapier through the draperies of sleep," Lindbergh explained later. A

change in air speed or an unexpected movement of the turn indicator brought him quickly alert. When the problem was solved and the danger was past, once more drowsiness would begin to work on the tired mind and numbed body of the Lone Eagle.

Night passed into day. To help stay alert, Lindbergh kept the windows open, letting in the snapping cold of the northern latitudes at which he was now flying. The Great Circle route he flew looked like a curved line on a map of Mercator projection. On the face of a globe, of course, it is a straight line and the shortest distance between two points. At one-hundred-mile intervals, Lindbergh made changes of direction in his course.

After eighteen hours, he was halfway to Paris. Nineteen hours passed, then twenty, then twenty-five, and still the Lone Eagle droned on. The Whirlwind engine purred smoothly, the *Spirit of St. Louis* responded nicely to every command. Then, in his twenty-seventh hour of flight, Lindbergh spotted black dots on the water below. Suddenly came the realization—they were *boats*—fishing boats. Land could not be far away.

Lindbergh dove down low over the boats, and after attracting the attention of a sailor, cut his engine and glided by, yelling out the window, "Which way is Ireland?" Receiving no reply from the first man he had seen in hours, Lindbergh straightened out and continued on his course. An hour passed, and then he sighted the coast of Ireland to the northeast. At first he didn't quite dare believe it was true, but on closer scrutiny he was convinced. There, two thousand feet below, lay Valentia and Dingle Bay on the southern tip of Ireland. He was right on course and two hours ahead of schedule!

Wide awake now, the drowsiness banished by his excitement and exulta-

---

In his twenty-seventh hour in the air, as he spotted fishing boats in the water below him, Lindbergh realized that land was near — his flight was nearly over.

63

tion, Lindbergh pointed the nose of the *Spirit of St. Louis* across County Kerry and St. George's Channel. Then, on to Cornwall, England, and then Plymouth, starting point for the Pilgrims some three hundred years before. The English Channel passed under his wings in less than an hour and at last the coast of France was safely reached. Once over the Cherbourg Peninsula, he had already earned the Orteig prize, but he flew onward up the valley of the Seine as night fell for the second time since he had left New York.

For the first time on this flight, Lindbergh's thoughts turned to food. He had brought along five sandwiches, and as he flew toward Paris, he nibbled one. By now it was dry and tasteless and he left the others untouched.

Suddenly a glow in the night sky rose ahead of the plane. Paris! In a few moments he was circling the Eiffel Tower before turning northeast to Le Bourget airfield. It took a few minutes before he definitely identified the airport and then came moments of panic as he found that his sense of "feel" for the controls had been numbed by the long hours behind him. The instinctive skill was there, however, and at exactly 10:24 P.M., Paris time, on May 21, 1927, Charles Lindbergh brought the *Spirit of St. Louis* to earth. The greatest flight in aviation history had ended.

Word of his approach had been flashed to Paris. By the time he arrived, a crowd of more than 100,000 enthusiastic Frenchmen were waiting at Le Bourget to welcome the Lone Eagle. After rolling to a stop, Lindbergh turned the plane around and peered out of his window into the darkness. Suddenly, out of the night, there appeared a great wave of humanity rushing headlong for his plane. He quickly cut his

The Spirit of St. Louis *at Le Bourget field outside Paris shortly after Lindbergh completed his historic solo transatlantic flight on May 21, 1927.*

motor to prevent any danger to the screaming crowd that engulfed the *Spirit of St. Louis*. As Lindbergh opened his cockpit door, he was greeted by scores of hands which lifted him bodily to the shoulders of the crowd.

At last a French aviator took Lindbergh's helmet and jammed it on the head of an unlucky American who happened to be in the crowd. At once the American became the center of attention and was quickly hoisted to the shoulders of the wildly cheering mob. Taking advantage of this opportunity, Lindbergh slipped away unnoticed to a hangar on the other side of the field. This was to be only the beginning of the adulation and acclaim bestowed on the weary flier in the weeks ahead.

Taken to the United States Embassy, Lindbergh became the guest of Ambassador Herrick. There followed a week of banquets, testimonial dinners, visits, receptions, and personal appearances before an adoring French populace. Messages of congratulation poured in from kings and presidents. At the request of the United States State Department, he flew to Brussels on May 28, and to London the following day. At both capitals there were receptions for him similar to the one that had

From a balcony in Paris, Charles Lindbergh (left) and United States Ambassador to France Myron Herrick (right) smile at a cheering crowd.

Two days after the Paris landing, Lindbergh circles over London (right) looking for a landing place.

taken place in Paris. On May 31, he flew the *Spirit of St. Louis* to Gosport, England, where it was dismantled, crated, and placed aboard the cruiser USS *Memphis*, which had been sent by President Coolidge. On June 3, in a borrowed Royal Air Force pursuit plane, Lindbergh flew back to Paris and from there to Cherbourg where he boarded the *Memphis* for the return journey to the United States.

On Saturday, June 11, 1927, the cruiser steamed slowly up the Potomac River to the Navy Yard dock in Washington, D.C. There a tumultous welcome awaited the returning hero. His mother, who had spent the previous night with the Coolidges, met him at the ship. Later, at the base of the Washington Monument, President Coolidge presented him with the Distinguished Flying Cross.

Charles Lindbergh received an enthusiastic reception when he returned to the United States after his flight. Upper left, his return to New York; right and lower left, Washington, D.C., where he received the Distinguished Flying Cross.

The following Monday, he flew to New York for the greatest welcoming parade in that city's history. Some 1800 tons of paper, confetti, and ticker tape streamed down from skyscrapers all along his route. His four days in New York were a continuation of the round of testimonials that had begun in Paris. At last, Raymond Orteig himself presented Lindbergh with the $25,000 Orteig Prize.

On June 17, 1927, Charles Lindbergh flew in his plane back to the place where it all began—St. Louis. The people of that great city on the Mississippi turned out to give him as warm a reception as he had received anywhere. The hero had returned and the spirit of St. Louis, the city, reached out to welcome him and the little silver plane named in its honor.

And so the race was ended. The prize was won. The quiet, modest young man from the midwest was now the hero of the hour across the length and breadth of America—indeed around the world. The courage inherited from pioneer ancestors, the irresistible desire for adventure, the appreciation of science and things mechanical, the uncanny skill in flying—all these had combined to mold Charles Lindbergh into the greatest flier of the age.

Far left, ticker-tape parade honoring Lindbergh in New York. Left, he is presented with the Orteig Prize.

The Later Years of a Hero

Lindbergh expected that all the furor and glory would soon die away. He was principally concerned with the promotion of aviation in the United States and he hoped he could soon escape from the public eye.

Such was not to be the case, however. The American public had taken him into their hearts. A mountain was named for him, as were thousands of babies. Dozens of poems and songs were written for him and he received scores of marriage proposals. Medals, gifts, and honors continued to flow in from across the country and around the world.

In July, just a few weeks after returning from Europe, Lindbergh began a tour of the United States in the *Spirit of St. Louis*, under the sponsorship of the Guggenheim Fund and the United States Department of Commerce. In three months he flew more than 22,000 miles, stopped in more than 80 cities, was guest at 69 dinners, and rode nearly 1300 miles in parades. He and his plane were seen by some thirty million people.

On December 13, 1927, he set off on another history-making trip, this time to Mexico City. He made the 2100-mile flight from Washington, D.C., to the Mexican capital in twenty-seven hours and fifteen minutes. While making plans for the journey with the Ambassador to Mexico, Dwight Morrow, he had met twenty-one-year-old Anne Spencer Morrow, the Ambassador's daughter. They saw each other often during the following months.

This 1928 photo shows Anne Spencer Morrow, daughter of the United States Ambassador to Mexico, who was to become the wife of Charles Lindbergh.

Mexican-American relations at the time were quite strained and Lindbergh's visit did much to improve the situation. He then continued on to visit fourteen Latin American countries, where tremendous crowds greeted him at every stop. He returned to St. Louis by way of Cuba.

On April 30, 1928, Lindbergh made his last flight in the *Spirit of St. Louis.* On that day, he flew from St. Louis to Washington, D.C., where he formally presented the plane to the Smithsonian Institution. He had often used the personal pronoun "we" when referring to himself and his plane. As he left the little silver plane for the last time, it was almost as if he were parting with a close personal friend.

A year after leaving his mechanical partner, Lindbergh took another partner—this one for life. On May 26, 1929, he married Anne Morrow, the pretty, dark-haired girl he had met in New York and courted in Mexico. She was a perfect match for Charles and shared the same enthusiasm for aviation. He taught her to fly and together they roamed the world in the years ahead. She became his navigator, co-pilot, and radio operator.

On Anne's birthday, June 22, 1930, Charles Augustus Lindbergh, Jr. was born. A year later, Anne and Charles left for the Orient in a pontoon monoplane they had named the *Sirius.* The couple flew across the desolate wastes of northern Canada to the Arctic, then curved down to Kamchatka, Japan, and

Far left, Mr. and Mrs. Charles Lindbergh in front of the Sirius, *the plane in which they flew to the Orient in 1931. Left, the* Sirius *is shown flying over frozen mountain peaks in Alaska during the trip.*

In February, 1929, Lindbergh flew the first airmail flight between Miami, Florida and Panama. The photograph shows his return flight, accompanied by three escort planes.

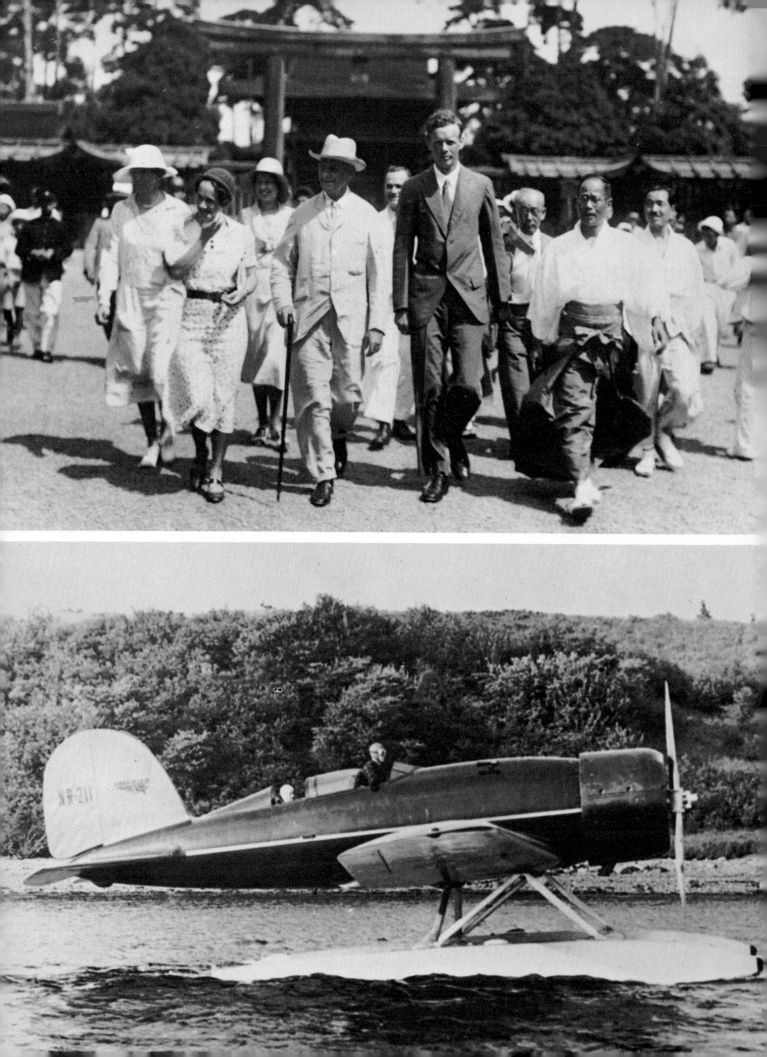

then over to China. On October 5, Anne's father died and the couple cut short their journey to return home.

In February of 1932, the Lindberghs moved into their new home near Hopewell, New Jersey. It was a large house, standing on some 400 acres of rolling woodland. This home was destined to be the scene of terrible tragedy in the weeks ahead.

On the night of May 1, 1932, baby Charles was taken from his crib. The kidnapper became the subject of the greatest manhunt in American history.

People everywhere were shocked and saddened by the terrible crime. Prayers were said throughout the nation for the safe return of the child.

Two and a half months later, the baby's body was found in a shallow grave not far from the Lindbergh home. He had apparently been killed within a few moments after being taken from his crib. The ransom had been paid in vain.

In August of 1932, another son was born to the Lindberghs. He was given the name Jon Morrow Lindbergh.

In July of the following year, Charles and Anne made a long scientific flight, testing new instruments, surveying possible commercial airline routes, and making a bacteria study over Greenland. They arrived home just before Christmas, having visited Iceland, Europe, Africa, and South America.

Franklin Delano Roosevelt was now President of the United States, and in February of 1934 he declared all airmail contracts null and void because of alleged irregularities. Lindbergh, now affiliated with Trans World Airlines, was angered by the action and sent telegrams to the President protesting the decision. This was the beginning of a personal "war" between these two strong-willed men.

The manhunt for the kidnapper of the Lindbergh baby had continued and finally, on September 19, 1934, the police tracked him down. The man's name was Bruno Richard Hauptmann, a German who had entered this country illegally in 1923. He was found guilty after the most sensational trial of the century. On April 3, 1936, still protesting his innocence, Hauptmann was executed in the electric chair. Meanwhile, Congress had passed the so-called "Lindbergh Law," which made kidnapping a federal offense. Kidnapping in the United States declined sharply after this law was passed.

In the early 1930's, Lindbergh had become interested in the medical research being conducted by Dr. Alexis Carrel, a former Nobel Prize winner. Dr. Carrel was conducting experiments at the Rockefeller Institute of Medical Research on the problem of keeping human organs alive outside the body.

During their 1931 flight to the Orient, Mr. and Mrs. Lindbergh visited the Meiji Shrine in Tokyo (top).
In 1933, the Lindberghs land at Halifax, Nova Scotia, during aerial survey flight from the State of Maine to Greenland.

Many of the problems were mechanical, and soon Lindbergh was using his amazing ingenuity and technical knowledge to devise a "perfusion pump" with which to revive life in organs removed from the body.

The sensationalism of the Hauptmann trial, the constant invasion of their privacy, and crank threats to baby Jon, convinced the Lindberghs that they must go abroad until the publicity died down.

They arrived in England on the last day of 1935, where they lived until the spring of 1938. During that time the couple made numerous flights to Europe, India, and North Africa.

These were the years during which Hitler's Nazi regime was busily preparing for the conquest of Europe. At the request of the United States military attaché in Berlin, Air Marshal Goering invited Lindbergh to view first-hand the German air progress. Lindbergh, of course, reported his findings to American military intelligence. He made several visits to Germany and was greatly impressed by the ever-growing might of the *Luftwaffe*. He became convinced that no combination of European allies could stand for long against the might of German air power.

Early in 1939, the Lindberghs returned to America. War was brewing in Europe and Charles felt that the United States should stay out of it. For two

Lindbergh is shown here visiting a military airport in Germany in 1936.

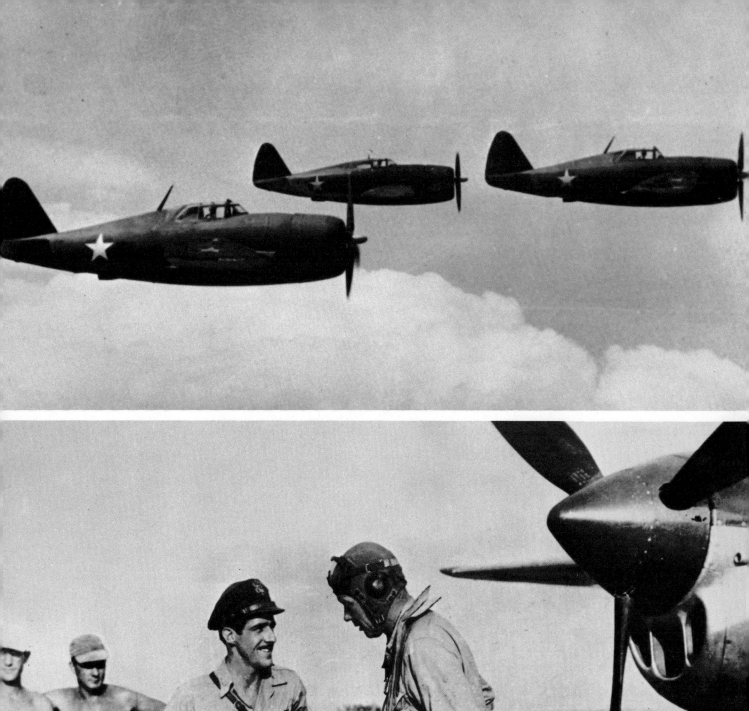

years he urged American isolationism, but at the same time continued to work for increased American military strength. In early 1941, he became a member of the America First Committee, which included such people as Henry Ford, Captain Eddie Rickenbacker, and Norman Thomas, the perpetual Socialist presidential candidate. This group was opposed to the foreign policy of the Roosevelt administration. After a further falling-out with the President, Lindbergh resigned his commission in the Army Air Corps Reserve.

On December 7, 1941, the Japanese attack on Pearl Harbor plunged America into war. Now there was only one foreign policy—victory. The Roosevelt administration refused to restore Lindbergh's commission, so he plunged himself into the war effort as a civilian. He became a technical consultant for the Ford Company, which was building the huge B-24 Liberator bombers. He also performed high-altitude tests in the P-47 Thunderbolt fighters. Later he became a test pilot, aeronautical engineer, and instructor at United Aircraft.

In the spring of 1944, he went to the Pacific as a technical consultant to study combat problems. Despite his age of forty-two, he flew more than fifty combat missions. It was not according to military and international law, of course, for a civilian to fly combat missions. But base commanders conveniently looked the other way when he climbed into a P-38 and trailed along on military missions. His major contributions were his experiments, which resulted in a 500-mile increase in the flying range for the P-38 Lightnings.

During World War II, Lindbergh, as a technical consultant for the Ford Company, made test flights in P-47 Thunderbolt fighter planes (top). During test flights for United Aircraft in 1945, Lindbergh was based in the Pacific (bottom). Left, a United States plane strafes a Japanese installation.

In mid-1944, Charles Lindbergh was flying P-38 Lightning fighters with the United States Fifth Air Force in the Pacific. Although a civilian, he had been sent to study combat problems—and what better way was there to study such problems than under actual combat conditions? Despite the fact that he could be shot as a spy if he were downed and captured, Lindbergh flew some fifty missions during his tour.

At the completion of each mission, mechanics were amazed to find that Lindbergh's plane had much more gas left in its tanks than the others. Seventeen years before, on his historic flight from New York to Paris, Lindbergh's life had depended upon economy of fuel consumption. This economy had become a habit with him and in 1944 he was still applying this habit to all his flights. By "leaning out" his fuel mixture and fiddling with his propeller "pitch" settings, Lindbergh had been able to extend the range of the P-38 more than 500 miles. This information was passed by official message to all other P-38 units in the area.

One day, Lindbergh and three officers of the Four Hundred and Seventy Fifth Fighter Group took off on a bombing mission from their base at Biak, near the western tip of New Guinea. Their target was the Japanese stronghold at Palau—previously considered beyond the range of P-38's.

The Japanese at Palau were dumbfounded when the four P-38's screamed across their airfield dropping bombs and firing machine guns at everything in sight. Before the Japanese could recover from their surprise, the Americans had destroyed three planes, caused other damage to ground installations, and were on their way home. One Japanese Zero which managed to take off was also shot down. All four Americans returned safely to their base at Biak.

The lessons in fuel economy, learned so many years before over the Atlantic, had paid more dividends for Lindbergh and his country in the skies above the Pacific.

After the war he served in many capacities and on various governmental committees in the field of aviation. In 1954, President Eisenhower nominated him for appointment to the rank of brigadier general in the United States Air Force Reserve. The appointment was confirmed two months later. In September of that same year, his mother died in Detroit after a long illness.

Today, Charles and Anne Lindbergh live in Darien, Connecticut. The former "Lone Eagle" is a consultant for Pan American Airways and a director of the World Wildlife Fund. He also continues his interest in medical research and spends time at the Navy Laboratory in Bethesda, Maryland. Four other

Far left, a 1947 photograph showing Lindbergh (second from right) and Jimmy Doolittle (right) inspecting a Navy pilotless aircraft. Left, Lindbergh after his 1954 appointment as brigadier general.

children, now grown, were born to the Lindberghs—two girls, Anne and Reeve, and two boys, Land and Scott.

At last Charles Lindbergh has achieved a measure of the privacy he so longed for in the years following his historic flight. In his middle age, he is generally unrecognized in his travels around the country. Discourteous crowds no longer dog his every step.

One day, not long ago, he made a quiet pilgrimage to the Smithsonian Institution in Washington, D.C. With scores of other tourists, he gazed fondly up at the little silver monoplane suspended from the ceiling. Outside, a huge jet airliner shrieked skyward, carrying more than a hundred passengers on a scheduled flight to Le Bourget airfield in Paris. It is a routine flight in this day and age. Perhaps some of the passengers on that jet remembered, however, that more than forty years ago a young man in a silver plane blazed that very path on wings of destiny.

Left, Lindbergh on a 1954 visit to Texas. Right, a 1957 visit by Brigadier General Charles A. Lindbergh (center) to Cape Canaveral, Florida, prior to a test launching of an intermediate-range ballistic missile.

Summary

For thirty-three and a half hours on a fateful Friday and Saturday in May, 1927, the world held its breath. Across the United States, people prayed, or crossed their fingers, or simply wished good luck for the young man flying alone in a small airplane over the vastness of the Atlantic Ocean. He flew in skies hitherto unknown to man and for a distance never before attempted.

It was a moment unique in the history of man—a moment of destiny beyond which lay new horizons and a new dimension. Aviation had not yet caught the imagination of the masses. It was a toy or a tool of war, with no practical application to the needs of man. At that point, a lone man showed the world what could be done. Ten years earlier, it had been an impossibility. Ten years later it would become commonplace. But at that moment, the dreams of man rode with Charles Lindbergh and his *Spirit of St. Louis*.

The clean-cut American youth who was pulled bodily from his plane by a mass of screaming, cheering Parisians, became a hero.

Today, when transcontinental and transoceanic flights are routine occurrences, the huge machines and the trained teams to run them have dwarfed the individual. The days have passed when a flight to anywhere on the globe will quicken the pulse of a generation. But the challenge of progress, the quest for yet broader horizons have projected man into space. Much of the impetus of space exploration derives from that moment when a lone flier fired the imagination of mankind.

Bibliography

ALLEN, FREDERICK LEWIS. *Only Yesterday*. New York: Harper, 1931.

"American Epic." *Time*, September 14, 1953.

ANDERSSON, INGVAR. *A History of Sweden*. London: Weidenfeld & Neiolson, 1956.

"Anne Morrow Lindbergh. Her Life Story in Pictures." *McCalls*, October, 1956.

BEAMISH, RICHARD. *The Story of Lindbergh, The Lone Eagle*. New York: International Press, 1927.

BRUNO, HARRY A. "Lindbergh, the Famous Unknown." *Saturday Evening Post*, October 21, 1933.

————. *Wings Over America*. New York: McBride, 1942.

COLE, WAYNE S. *America First, The Battle Against Intervention, 1940-1941*. University of Wisconsin Press, 1953.

COUGHLIN, G. "When Lindbergh Saved The Day For Me." *Reader's Digest*, February, 1958.

CROIX, ROBERT. *They Flew The Atlantic*. London: Muller, 1958.

DALGLIESH, ALICE. *Ride on the Wind*. New York: Scribner's, 1956.

DAVIS, R. "Lindbergh Still Solos in Anonymity." *Newsweek*, December 5, 1949.

FIFE, GEORGE BUCHANAN. *Lindbergh, The Lone Eagle*. New York: A. L. Burt, 1927.

FISHWICK, MARSHALL. *American Heroes, Myth and Reality*. Washington: Public Affairs Press, 1954.

FOLWELL, WILLIAM WATTS. *A History of Minnesota*. Minnesota Historical Society, 1926.

FRASER, CHELSEA. *Heroes of the Air*. New York: Thomas Crowell, 1940.

GAMM, E. K. "Wine of the Gods." *Saturday Review*, September 12, 1953.

GUGGENHEIM, HARRY. *The Seven Skies*. New York: Putnams, 1930.

HAINES, LYNN and DORA B. *The Lindberghs*. New York: Vanguard and/or McCalls Magazine, 1931.

"Headlines of the Twenties." *Life*, January 2, 1950.

HICKS, JOHN D. *The Populist Revolt*. University of Wisconsin Press, 1951.

HOFSTADTER, RICHARD. *The Age of Reform*. New York: Knopf, 1955.

HOOLEY, ARTHUR, ed. *The Spirit of St. Louis, 100 poems*. New York: Doran, 1927.

KEYHOE, DONALD. *Flying with Lindbergh*. New York: Putnams, 1928.

LAITEN, J. "Lucky to be Lindy." *Colliers*, March 30, 1956.

LEEUEU, HENDRIK. *Conquest of the Air*. New York: Vantage, 1960.

LEHMAN, M. "How Lindbergh Gave a Lift to Rocketry." *Life*, October 4, 1963.

"Lindbergh and the Luftwaffe." *American Mercury*, April, 1956.

LINDBERGH, ANNE MORROW. *Listen The Wind*. New York: Harcourt, 1938.

———. *North to the Orient*. New York: Harcourt, 1935.

LINDBERGH, CHARLES. "Fourth Dimension of Survival." *Saturday Review*, February 27, 1954.

———. "Is Civilization Progress?" *Reader's Digest*, July, 1964.

———. "Lesson From the Wright Brothers." *Aviation Week*, December 26, 1949.

———. *Of Flight & Life*. New York: 1948.

———. "Our Best Chance to Survive." *Saturday Evening Post*, July 17, 1954.

———. "Salute to 1927 Heroes." *Aviation Week*, May 19, 1952.

———. "Skeptics 10 Years Ago, Too." *United States News & World Report*, February 23, 1951.

———. *The Spirit of St. Louis*. New York: Scribner's, 1953.

———. "Thoughts of a Combat Pilot." *Saturday Evening Post*, October 2, 1954.

———. "*We*." New York: Grosset, 1927.

LINDBERGH, CHARLES and ALEXIS CARREL. *The Culture of Organs*. New York: Hoeber, 1938.

"Lindbergh." *St. Louis Globe Democrat Magazine*, June 19, 1927.

Lindbergh the Flier of Little Falls. Little Falls, Minn.: Little Falls High School, 1928.

LYMAN, L. D. "The Lindbergh I Know." *Saturday Evening Post*, April 4, 1953.

MILLER, FRANCIS. *Lindbergh, his story in pictures*. New York: Putnams, 1929.

NEUBERGER, RICHARD. "The Hero Had a Father." *Esquire*, September, 1937.

NICOLSON, HAROLD. *Dwight Morrow*. New York: Harcourt, Brace, 1935.

NIEBUR, REINHOLD. *The Self and the Dramas of History*. New York: Scribner's, 1955.

"Obituary of Mrs. Charles Augustus Lindbergh." *Time*, September 20, 1954 and *Newsweek*, September 20, 1954.

O'BRIAN, P. J. *The Lindberghs, The Story of a Distinguished Family*. New York: International Press, 1935.

PAULDING, G. "Thoughtful Hero." *Reporter*, October 27, 1953.

PAYNE, G. "Prelude to Greatness." *Coronet*, September, 1955.

PUDNEY, JOHN. *Six Great Aviators*. London: Hamilton, 1955.

PUTNAM, G. P. *Soaring Wings, A Biography of Amelia Earhart*. New York: Harcourt, Brace, 1939.

REEVES, EARL. *Lindbergh Flies On!* 1930.

REYNOLDS, QUENTIN. *They Fought For The Sky*. New York: Rinehart, 1957.

ROSS, WALTER S. *The Last Hero*. New York: Harper & Row, 1968.

———. "Where Did Charles Lindbergh Go?" *Esquire*, October, 1963.

SKARDON, J. A. "Flight From Fame." *Coronet*, July, 1957.

SMITH, HENRY LADD. *Airways, The History of Commercial Aviation in the U.S.* New York: Knopf, 1942.

"Spirit of Lindbergh." *Newsweek*, November 29, 1954.

The Flight of Captain Charles A. Lindbergh from New York to Paris, May 20-21, As compiled from the Official Records of the Department of State. U.S. Government Printing Office, 1927.

TOZER, E. "Lindbergh's Amazing Airplane." *Popular Science*, May, 1957.

VAN EVERY, DALE and MORRIS DE HAVEY TRACY. *Charles Lindbergh*. New York: Appleton, 1927.

WALLER, GEORGE. *Kidnap; the story of the Lindbergh case*. New York: Dial, 1961.

———. "Lindbergh. The Little Plane, The Big Atlantic." *New York Times Magazine*, May 20, 1952.

WECTER, DIXON. *The Hero in America*. New York: Scribner's, 1941.

WEST, JAMES E. "The Lone Scout of the Sky." Boy Scouts of America, 1927.

WHIPPLE, SIDNEY, ed. *The Trial of Bruno Richard Hauptmann*. New York: Doubleday, 1937.

Index